# Wuthering Heights

## Emily Brontë

Abridged and adapted by Janice Greene

Illustrated by James McConnell

A PACEMAKER CLASSIC

FEARON/JANUS/QUERCUS
Belmont, California

**Simon & Schuster Supplementary Education Group**

## Other Pacemaker Classics

*The Adventures of Huckleberry Finn*
*The Adventures of Tom Sawyer*
*A Christmas Carol*
*Crime and Punishment*
*The Deerslayer*
*Dr. Jekyll and Mr. Hyde*
*Ethan Frome*
*Frankenstein*
*Great Expectations*
*Jane Eyre*
*The Jungle Book*
*The Last of the Mohicans*
*Moby Dick*
*The Moonstone*
*The Red Badge of Courage*
*Robinson Crusoe*
*The Scarlet Letter*
*A Tale of Two Cities*
*The Three Musketeers*
*The Time Machine*
*Treasure Island*
*20,000 Leagues Under the Sea*
*Two Years Before the Mast*

Library of Congress Catalog Card Number: 90-85004

ISBN 0–8224–9357–8

Printed in the United States of America

1. 9 8 7 6 5 4

# Contents

# The Principal Characters in *Wuthering Heights*

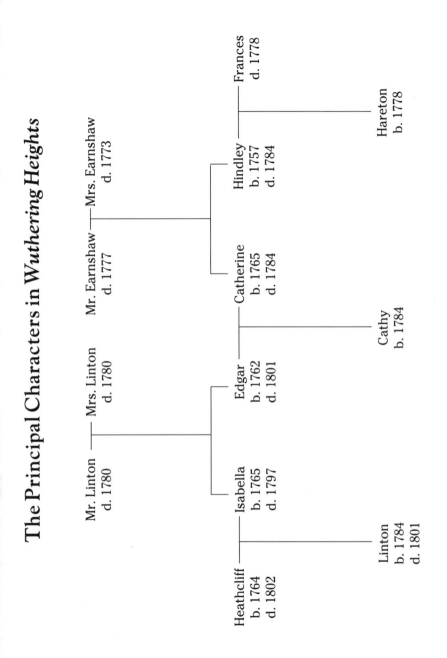

# 1 On the Moors

In the winter of 1801, I rented a house in a lonely corner of northern England. One day, soon after I moved in, I set out on a walk. I wanted to visit my new landlord, Mr. Heathcliff. I was struck by the beauty of the bleak, empty countryside. The wild Yorkshire moors were very lonely, indeed. It seemed to be a perfect place for someone who wanted to be away from people. It was just the right sort of place for me. And Mr. Heathcliff chose to live here, too. So I thought that he and I must be very much alike.

Mr. Heathcliff's farm was called Wuthering Heights. Next to the sturdy house on the hilltop, I could see a few stunted firs. I noticed the way the small trees slanted. So I could imagine the power of the north wind during stormy weather. When I rode up on my horse, Mr. Heathcliff was standing by the gate. I said, "Mr. Heathcliff?"

He said not a word. There was a look of suspicion in his black eyes.

"I am Mr. Lockwood," I said. "I am the man who will be renting Thrushcross Grange. . . ."

"Walk in," said Mr. Heathcliff, through closed teeth. He spoke the words as if he were cursing. Then he called, "Joseph, take Mr. Lockwood's horse and bring up some wine."

The servant Joseph was an old man, but he looked strong. He gave me a hard look. He said, "Lord help us," as he led my horse away.

As we walked to the house, I looked up at the door. The wood over the door had been carved. I read the words: "Hareton Earnshaw," and the date "1500."

The house looked like any other farmer's house. But Mr. Heathcliff did not look like a farmer. He looked like a dark-skinned gypsy. He dressed like a gentleman, but he was not really very neat or clean. He was a handsome man, but sad-looking. I thought he was afraid to show his feelings.

But I should not have thought such things about Mr. Heathcliff. I did not know him. *I* was the one who was afraid to show feelings.

The summer before, I was staying by the sea. I met a wonderful young woman. I never told her I loved her. But anyone could see I was deeply in love. At last one day she saw how much I cared for her. I could tell by the way she looked at me. You have never seen a look so sweet. And what did I do? I turned coldly back into myself, like a snail.

After that, every time she looked at me, I turned away. At last the poor thing left. People began talking about how I had no heart. Only I knew how wrong they were.

Mr. Heathcliff and I sat down. But Joseph had not come with the wine. So Mr. Heathcliff got up and went to the cellar to get it himself. I was left with three rough-looking dogs. They watched every move I made.

I didn't want to feel their teeth, but I felt like making fun of them. I began to wink and make faces. Suddenly one of the dogs sprang at my knees. I pushed her back. I pulled the table between us. But now six dogs, large and small, came from other parts of the house. They bit at my heels and coat. I fought them with a poker and called for help.

At last a big, red-faced woman came out of the kitchen with a frying pan. She yelled at the dogs and swung her frying pan at them. By the time Heathcliff came into the room, every dog had gone.

Mr. Heathcliff gave me a hard look. He said, "What the devil is the matter?"

"Those dogs!" I said. "You might as well leave a man with a family of tigers!"

Mr. Heathcliff said, "Come, Mr. Lockwood. Take a little wine. My dogs and I are not used to people. We don't know how to make others feel at home."

Mr. Heathcliff told me all about the place I had chosen to live. I liked talking with him very much. I said I might come again the next day. To this, Mr. Heathcliff said nothing. I didn't think he really wanted to see me again. But I planned to be back, just the same.

The next afternoon was misty and cold. I walked the four miles to Wuthering Heights. As I arrived at the house, it began to snow.

I knocked and knocked on the door. There was no answer. At last, Joseph called from the barn, "What do you want? Mr. Heathcliff's here if you want to speak to him."

I called, "Can't anyone open the door?"

Joseph said, "There's no one inside but the missis. And she'll not open it if you knock all day."

At last a young man came up. He led me into the house. The table was set for dinner. Sitting near the table was the "missis."

She looked up at me but she did not move.

"What a cold day, Mrs. Heathcliff," I said.

She didn't even open her mouth. She only looked at me in a cool way.

"Sit down," said the young man. "He'll be in soon."

I sat. Now I could see Mrs. Heathcliff well. She was quite young and beautiful. Her hair was gold. It hung in curls on her neck. She had a very pretty little face. But her face was full of anger and a terrible sadness.

I did not know what to make of the young man. He was dressed like a farm hand. He looked like a servant, but he did not act like one. He seemed very proud.

Mr. Heathcliff came into the room.

I said, "You see, sir, I have come, just as I said I would! I think I must stay for half an hour or so until the snow stops."

Mr. Heathcliff said, "Half an hour! It will last longer than that. And if you try to walk back, you could get lost in the marshes."

"Could you let one of the farm boys help me find my way?" I asked.

"No, I could not," he said.

"Oh!" I said. "Then I must make my own way."

Mr. Heathcliff said, "Umph!"

Dinner was on the table and we all sat down to eat. I said, "You are far away from the rest of the world here, Mr. Heathcliff. But I do think that with your kind lady here . . ."

"My kind lady!" said Mr. Heathcliff. He had an awful look on his face. "Where is she—my kind lady?"

Then it dawned on me. The young man was the woman's husband. This clown who eats his bread with dirty hands. How sad!

I turned to the young man and said, "Ah, I see now. You are the happy husband of this beautiful young woman."

This was worse than before. The young man turned red. He looked as if he wanted to hit me.

Mr. Heathcliff said, "I'm afraid you're wrong again. This young woman's husband is dead."

The young man turned to me. "My name is Hareton Earnshaw," he said. "And you'd better respect it!"

I began to feel quite out of place at this strange family dinner. When we had finished eating, I looked out the window. It was getting dark. The sky and hills were lost in a bitter swirl of wind and snow. I knew I would never find the road back home.

"I'm afraid I must stay the night," I said.

"I don't keep rooms for people," Mr. Heathcliff said. "You'll have to share a bed with Hareton or Joseph."

"I can sleep on a chair in this room," I said.

"No, no!" said Mr. Heathcliff. "I will not have people walking around the house while I cannot watch them."

This was more than I could bear. I took hold of a lantern. I said I would bring it back the next day. And I walked out the door.

Joseph called, "Mr. Heathcliff! He's taking the lantern! Hey, dogs! Hold him, hold him!"

Two large dogs jumped at me. They knocked me down. They didn't bite, but they wouldn't let me up. Heathcliff and Hareton laughed. I yelled at them. I was terribly angry. My nose began to bleed.

The big housekeeper came out. This was Zillah, who had helped me the day before. She said, "Look at the poor boy! Don't be so upset now! Come in and I'll take care of that. There now, hold still."

To stop my nosebleed, she threw some very cold water down my neck. I felt sick and dizzy. Now I knew I would have to stay the night. Zillah brought me inside. When I felt better, she led me to another room.

She told me to hide my candle as I walked. She said that Mr. Heathcliff did not like anyone to stay in this room.

# 2  A Bad Dream

In my room, I found several old books. One of them was a Testament. Inside it was written, "Catherine Earnshaw, her book." The date went back about 25 years.

On almost every page, this Catherine Earnshaw had written in the blank spaces and margins. I started to read:

*An awful Sunday! I wish my father were alive again. Hindley is awful. He can never take Father's place. And Hindley is so cruel to Heathcliff! Heathcliff and I are going to rebel.*

*It rained hard all day. We could not go to church. So Joseph made Heathcliff and me go upstairs with our prayer books. Hindley and his wife stayed downstairs by the fire. I'm sure they were doing anything but reading their Bibles. We sat upstairs with Joseph for three long hours.*

*But when my brother Hindley saw us coming downstairs, he said, "What, done already?" Then he turned to his wife. He said, "Frances, pull the boy's hair as he goes by. I'm sure I heard him snap his fingers."*

*Frances gave Heathcliff's hair a good strong pull. Then she went and sat on Hindley's knee. And there they sat like two babies. They could kiss and talk about nothing by the hour.*

*Heathcliff and I found a place to hide. But soon Joseph found us.*

*Joseph said, "Shame on you! Playing on a Sunday. And the master just buried!"*

*Hindley got up and led both of us into the back kitchen. I found this book and began to write. But Heathcliff has another idea. He thinks we should go out in the rain and walk on the moors. A good idea—how could we get any colder than we are now?*

I decided that Catherine and Heathcliff must have gone out in the rain. For the next time she wrote, she said:

*I never thought Hindley would ever make me cry so! My head hurts so much I cannot keep it on the pillow. Poor Heathcliff! Hindley says Heathcliff cannot eat at the table with us anymore. And he and I cannot play together. Hindley says my father is to blame, for letting Heathcliff have his way so long. (How dare he say that about Father!) Hindley says he will put Heathcliff in his place.*

My head began to nod. I sank back in bed, fell asleep, and began to dream.

In my dream, I heard a tree branch hitting against the window. I got up to stop the noise.

The window could not be opened, so I broke the glass with my fist. I reached out to take hold of the branch. Instead, my fingers closed on a small, ice-cold hand!

The full horror of the dream came over me. I tried to pull back my arm, but the hand grabbed at mine. A voice cried, "Let me in—let me in!"

I tried and tried to pull my hand away. I said, "Who are you?"

"I am Catherine," said the sad voice. "I've come home. I had lost my way on the moor!"

Still I could not pull my hand free. I was so afraid I turned cruel. I rubbed the hand on the broken glass. Blood ran down onto the sheets. Yet still the hand held me.

"Let me in!" cried the voice again.

At last I said, "How can I? Let me go, if you want to get in."

The hand let go. I pulled my hand free. As fast as I could, I covered the hole with books. But the voice outside would not be quiet.

I said, "Go away! I'll never let you in, not if you beg for 20 years!"

The voice said, "It *is* 20 years. I've been lost out here for 20 years!"

Then the books moved, as if she had pushed them. I yelled out loud, and woke up. All at once I heard footsteps. The door opened. Heathcliff said in a whisper, "Is anyone there?" It was clear he did not think anyone was in the room.

I knew he couldn't see me. But I thought I should tell him I was there. I sat up, making a noise. I said, "It is only I, sir. I had a bad dream. I called out in my sleep."

Heathcliff's hand shook so much he could not hold his candle. He put it on the table. "Who let you into this room?" he said. "Who was it? I'll turn them out of the house!"

I said, "It was your servant Zillah. And I don't care if you throw her out of the house. I think she wanted to be sure there were ghosts in the room. Well, there are! There was that awful little thing—that Catherine! I think she would have killed me if she had gotten in!"

As soon as I said these words, I was sorry. For Heathcliff had been in the book, too.

I said, "The truth is, sir, that I was reading these old books. And the name Catherine stayed in my mind as I fell asleep."

Heathcliff's voice was like thunder. "What can you mean by talking to me in this way? How—how dare you!"

He sank down on the bed. His breath came hard. I think he wiped a tear from his eye.

I said, "I cannot go to sleep again. I will walk in the yard until morning."

He said, "Take the candle, and go where you like. I will come out in a minute."

I started to leave. But I did not know which way to go. Then I saw Mr. Heathcliff pull open the window. He burst out in wild crying. He called, "Come in! Come in! Catherine, do come once more. Hear me *this* time, Catherine, at last!"

He seemed so terribly sad that I felt sorry for him. I went away. I wished I had not told him about my dream. After a while, I found my way to the kitchen. I was surprised to see Heathcliff there. It seemed he had just finished an angry scene with Zillah. The poor woman was drying her eyes with a corner of her apron.

I did not stay for breakfast. As soon as it was light, I went out into the fresh air. The day was clear and cold as ice.

Mr. Heathcliff led me across the moor. It was a good thing he did. The hills were like a white ocean of fallen snow. I would have lost my way many times.

At last I came to the house at Thrushcross Grange. The servants ran to meet me. They thought I had gotten lost and died during the night.

# 3 The "Dirty Little Child"

How quickly people change! At first I had wanted to be far away from people. That is why I came here. But now I wanted very much to talk to someone. I knew that one of the servants had lived here many years. Her name was Mrs. Nelly Dean. I began asking her about the people of Wuthering Heights. She was happy to tell me all she knew. But first she brought me something hot to eat, for I shook with cold. Then she sat down and started to tell me the story of Wuthering Heights.

Mrs. Dean began:

My mother was a servant at Wuthering Heights. So I spent most of my time there. I helped around the farm. I also took care of the children, and played with them.

At the time, Wuthering Heights belonged to old Mr. Earnshaw. One day he told his family he was going to Liverpool. He said he would bring each child a present. He asked them what they wanted.

Hindley, who was 14, wanted a fiddle. Catherine wanted a whip. She was not quite six, but she could ride any one of the horses.

He was gone three days. To the children it seemed a very long time. At last he arrived home. It was quite late and he was very tired.

He sank into a chair and opened up his coat. He said, "Look here, Wife! I've never seen such a thing in all my life. It's as dark as if it came from the devil. But you must take it as a gift from God."

We came up to look. It was a dirty little child. It looked around. It started speaking some strange words, over and over.

I was scared. Mrs. Earnshaw was very upset. She wanted to put the child out of the house.

Mr. Earnshaw tried to tell his wife what had happened. He was in Liverpool when he saw the child out on the streets. It had no home. Mr. Earnshaw could not find out who it belonged to. But he could not bear to leave it there, so he brought it home with him.

Well, Mrs. Earnshaw quickly told her husband what she thought of the whole thing. But, at last, she had nothing more to say.

Mr. Earnshaw told me to wash the dirty little boy and put him to bed with the children.

The children had been quiet. Now they came to get their presents. But Hindley's fiddle had been broken in his father's coat. He burst into tears. And while Mr. Earnshaw had been helping the boy, he

had lost Catherine's whip. So Catherine began to spit at the little thing—until her father hit her.

The children would not let the poor child in the room with them. I was just as cruel. I put him out on the stairs. I hoped he would be gone in the morning. But somehow he made his way to Mr. Earnshaw's room. Mr. Earnshaw found out I had left him on the stairs. He was angry at me and sent me home.

I didn't think Mr. Earnshaw meant for me to stay away. So a few days later, I came back to the house. I found they had named the child "Heathcliff." It was the name of a son who had died. The boy Heathcliff and Catherine were now close friends. But Hindley hated him. To tell the truth, I hated him, too.

Hindley and I were quite cruel to him. And Mrs. Earnshaw never protected him. I think Heathcliff had known a lot of cruelty. He never cried when Hindley hit him. If I pinched him, he never made a sound.

Mr. Earnshaw got terribly angry when he saw his son hurting Heathcliff. He could not bear to see anyone be cruel to the boy. He began to feel a deep love for Heathcliff.

Two years later, Mrs. Earnshaw died. And by this time, Hindley felt that Heathcliff had taken his place in his father's heart.

Heathcliff knew well how much Mr. Earnshaw cared for him. He knew he only had to speak and he would have what he wanted. But somehow he never seemed glad of the old man's love.

One day Mr. Earnshaw bought two horses at the fair. Heathcliff took the best-looking one. But it fell lame. So he said to Hindley, "You must change horses with me. I don't like mine. If you won't, I'll tell your father how you hit me this week. And I'll show him my arm. It's black and blue from the hand to the shoulder."

Hindley made a face. He hit Heathcliff on the ears.

Heathcliff said, "You'd better do what I say. Or I'll tell him what you did. Then *you'll* get hit."

Hindley picked up a piece of iron. He said, "Back off, dog!"

Heathcliff stood still. He said, "Throw it. I'll tell your father how you said you'd put me out of the house when he died. Then he'll put *you* out of the house."

Hindley threw it. It hit Heathcliff on the chest. He fell to the ground but got up quickly, breathing hard. His face was white.

If I had not stopped Heathcliff, he would have gone to Mr. Earnshaw right away.

Hindley said, "Take my horse, then! And I hope he breaks your neck. You can take from my father everything he has. But show him who you are—you child of the devil!"

I told Heathcliff he must not tell what happened. He agreed. He didn't really care. Once he had what he wanted, nothing else bothered him. I thought he didn't care about getting even with people. But I was quite wrong, as you will see.

In time, Mr. Earnshaw became weak and sick. He was often cross. Any little thing made him angry. But one thing would upset him most of all: if anyone said something bad about Heathcliff.

If Hindley was cruel to Heathcliff, Mr. Earnshaw got terribly angry. He would try to hit Hindley with his stick. But now he was not strong enough to do it. And that made him even angrier.

At the time, a curate from the nearby village of Gimmerton used to come out to teach the children. The curate told Mr. Earnshaw he should send Hindley to college. And so Hindley went away.

I hoped we would have peace in the house now, but we did not. It was mostly because of Catherine.

I've never seen a child act the way she did. Catherine would make us all angry 50 times a day. Her tongue never stopped. She was always singing and laughing. Then she would bother anyone else who would not do the same. She was wild and bad. But she had the prettiest eyes and the sweetest smile around. And I don't think she ever really meant to hurt people. She was much too close to Heathcliff. The worst thing we could do to Catherine was to keep him away from her.

Her wild ways made Mr. Earnshaw very angry. He hated the way Heathcliff would do anything she wanted. Heathcliff would only obey Mr. Earnshaw if *he* felt like it.

Then the hour came when Mr. Earnshaw left all his troubles on earth. It was a wild night outside. We were sitting around the fire. Catherine had been sick, so she was quiet for once. She leaned on her father's knee. Heathcliff lay on the floor. His head was in Catherine's lap.

Mr. Earnshaw said, "Why can't you always be such a good girl, Catherine?"

Catherine laughed. "Why can't you always be a good man, Father?" she said. But she saw this upset him. So she kissed his hand. She began singing very low. He fell asleep. We all kept quiet, so that he could sleep.

Then Joseph said he must wake Mr. Earnshaw. It was time for prayers and bed. He touched Mr. Earnshaw's arm. He brought the candle close to the old man's face.

I thought there must be something wrong. Joseph told the children to get up to bed—quickly.

But Catherine said, "I must say good night to Father first." Before we could stop her, she put her arms around his neck.

She cried out, "Oh, he's dead, Heathcliff! He's dead!"

Joseph sent me to get the doctor and the parson. When I came back, I went to the children's room. Catherine and Heathcliff were talking about their feelings for Mr. Earnshaw. No parson in the world could have talked about heaven as beautifully as they did. I began to cry. I wished we were all safe in heaven together.

# 4 The Lintons

Hindley came home for the funeral. And he surprised us all by bringing a wife home with him! Her name was Frances.

Hindley never told us who she was, or where she came from. So I think she had no name or money.

Frances seemed a very happy young woman. She loved the house and everything in it. But everything about Mr. Earnshaw's funeral upset her.

When the neighbors came to the house, she ran to her room. She said she could not bear to see people dressed in black. She kept asking me, "Are they gone yet?"

I asked her what was wrong. She said she did not know. But she was terribly afraid of dying.

This seemed silly to me. She was thin, but young, with fresh-looking skin. Her eyes were very bright. Still I could see that climbing the stairs made her breathe very hard. And she did cough quite a bit sometimes. But I didn't know what these signs meant.

Hindley had changed a lot in the three years he had been away. He was thinner and he dressed quite differently. His manner changed, too. On the day he came back, he told Joseph and me that we must no longer walk about the house. From then on, we must stay in the back kitchen and leave the rest of the house to him. As for Heathcliff, Hindley would not let him live in the house anymore. He had to live with the servants. And he could have no more lessons from the curate. Instead, Heathcliff must work on the farm.

At first, Heathcliff took Hindley's cruelty fairly well. After Catherine had her lessons, she would tell Heathcliff all she learned. And she worked or played with him in the fields. It seemed both children would grow up wild. Hindley did not care what they did, as long as they kept out of his way.

Often Heathcliff and Catherine would run off. They would spend all day playing on the moors. When they were punished later, they would only laugh. The curate might punish Catherine by giving her many chapters in her books to learn by heart. And Joseph might hit Heathcliff until his arm was tired. But Heathcliff and Catherine forgot everything as soon as they were together.

One Sunday evening, Catherine and Heathcliff had been sent out of the sitting room. They had made some noise, or done some other little wrong. When I went to call them to dinner, they were gone.

We looked all over the house. We looked in the yard and the barn. But we couldn't find them anywhere. Hindley was terribly angry. He told us to lock the doors. No one must let them in that night.

Everyone went to bed. But I could not lie down. I opened my window and I listened. I decided that I was going to let them in. I didn't care what Hindley said.

Soon I heard steps coming down the road. I ran outside. It was Heathcliff. He was alone.

"Where is Miss Catherine?" I said.

"At Thrushcross Grange," Heathcliff said. "Catherine and I went to have a look at the Lintons. We wanted to see if they spent *their* Sundays standing in cold corners.

"We ran all the way to Thrushcross Grange. I beat Catherine in the race. She was barefoot. You'll have to look for her shoes in the bog tomorrow. We went along a path, right up to their house. We looked in the window. It was beautiful inside! It was all red—the carpet, and the chairs and tables. The ceiling was pure white. In the middle of the ceiling was a shower of glass-drops. They were shining with soft candles.

"Old Mr. and Mrs. Linton were not there. Edgar and his sister had the room to themselves. And were they happy in that beautiful place? We would have been in heaven! But guess what those good children were doing? Isabella was screaming at one end of the room. Edgar was crying by the fireplace. They had been fighting over a little dog. The fools!

"Catherine and I laughed. I would never wish for something Catherine wanted. I would never trade my place here for Edgar Linton's. Not even if I could throw Joseph off the roof. Or paint the house with Hindley's blood!"

I said, "Hush, hush! You still have not told me. Why is Catherine not here?"

Heathcliff said, "I told you we laughed. The Lintons heard us. They cried for their mama and papa. So we ran away.

"I had Catherine by the hand. But all at once she fell down. She said, 'Run, Heathcliff! They have let the dog loose, and he's got me!'

"A bulldog had her by the foot. I grabbed a stone. The dog let go of Catherine's foot, and I tried to push the stone down its throat. Just then a servant ran up. When he saw Catherine, he picked her up and carried her toward the house. I followed them, grumbling and cursing.

"Old Mr. Linton called from the house, 'What did the dog catch?'

"The servant said, 'A little girl, sir. And there's a boy here, too. He looks like a real out-and-outer.'

"The Lintons came up to look at us. Edgar said to his mother, 'That's Miss Earnshaw. And look how the dog has bitten her!'

"Mrs. Linton said, 'Why, my dear, it *is* Miss Earnshaw. But why is she out here with this awful gypsy boy? Did you ever hear a boy talk like this? I'm shocked that my children should have heard him.'

"I started to curse again. They told the servant to take me away. He dragged me through the garden and pushed me through the gate.

"But as soon as I could, I ran back to the house and stared in the window. I wanted to see if Catherine was all right.

"She sat on the sofa. A servant washed her foot. Then they dried and combed her beautiful hair. They gave her things to eat and drink. She gave some food to their little dog—and pinched his nose. They all smiled at her. She is so much better than they are. She is so much better than anyone on earth, isn't she, Nelly?"

I said more would come of this day than he thought. How right I was!

# 5 A Sad, Angry Young Man

Catherine stayed at Thrushcross Grange five weeks. By that time her foot was quite well. And she began acting more like a little lady. What a surprise when she came home! She wore a hat, and her hair was in curls. How fine she looked in her new silk dress and shiny shoes.

When she saw Heathcliff, she ran to him. She looked very different from her friend now. He was dirty from working every day on the farm. And he always had an angry face in those days.

She kissed him many times on the cheek. Then she laughed. "Why, Heathcliff," she said, "how rough and cross you look! But maybe that's because I'm used to being with Edgar and Isabella Linton."

"I will not be laughed at. I cannot bear it!" said Heathcliff.

"I didn't mean to laugh at you," Catherine said. "It was only that you looked so strange. If you would wash your face and brush your hair, you'd look fine. But you are so dirty!"

Heathcliff said, "You should not have touched me, then! I like to be dirty!" He ran out of the room. He stayed away from the house all that day.

The next morning, the family went to church. I was busy in the kitchen. Edgar and Isabella Linton were coming to the house after church, and there would be a party. While I was working, Heathcliff came in. He said, "Nelly, help me clean up. I'm going to be good!"

"I will indeed!" I said. "You'll be quite handsome! Edgar Linton will look like nothing next to you."

Heathcliff said sadly, "But I don't have light hair and skin like he has. And I don't dress as well or act as well. Nor do I have his chance of being rich."

"And you don't cry for your mama at every turn!" I said. "Oh, Heathcliff, have more spirit! Look at yourself in the mirror. You look as angry as a dog who is ready to bite. A good heart should have a handsome face."

I talked on and on, trying to cheer him up. Soon he was washed and clean. And at last he lost his frown.

We heard the family come back from church. Edgar and Isabella were with them. I led Heathcliff out to meet them. But when Hindley saw Heathcliff, he said, "Get upstairs! You can't stay down here with the others. Look at you! Fixing yourself up, are you? Such fine hair you have! I'll pull it a little longer!"

Edgar said, "I think his hair is long enough already. It's over his eyes, like a horse's mane."

I don't believe Edgar meant to be mean. But Heathcliff was terribly angry. He grabbed the first thing he could put his hand on—a bowl of hot applesauce. He threw it at Edgar's face.

Hindley grabbed Heathcliff and pulled him upstairs. I grabbed a dishcloth and rubbed Edgar's face—hard.

Catherine turned to Edgar. She said, "Why did you say that to Heathcliff? Now Hindley will beat him! I hate for him to be beaten!"

Isabella was crying. So was Edgar. He said, "I didn't say anything to him. I promised Mama I wouldn't say a word to him. And I didn't!"

Catherine's voice was cold. She said, "Well, don't cry. And you stop crying, too, Isabella. Nobody's hurt *you*."

Hindley came back into the room. He said, "Come, children. Take your seats."

Everyone sat down at the table. After a little while, the Lintons began to have a good time. Catherine talked and laughed with them. But at times I could see that she was close to tears. As soon as she could, she went off to be with Heathcliff.

I saw Heathcliff later that night. He was very quiet. I asked him what he was thinking about.

Heathcliff said, "I'm thinking about how I will pay Hindley back. I don't care how long it takes. But I must pay him back."

I said, "You must not think such things! It is for God to punish. We must learn to forgive."

Heathcliff said, "Let me alone, Nelly. I must plan it out. While I think of it, I don't feel my pain."

All at once, Mrs. Dean stopped telling her story. She said, "Oh, Mr. Lockwood. See how late it is! I have been keeping you up far too long. I could have made the story much shorter."

When she got up, I held her arm. "Do sit still, Mrs. Dean," I said. "Stay another half hour. You've done right to tell the story slowly. Please go on."

"I will go on, if you like," Mrs. Dean answered. "But I will skip to the next summer. The summer of 1778, almost 23 years ago."

It was a fine June day when Hindley's son was born. I was in the fields, helping with the hay. One of the servant girls came running from the house with the news.

She said, "Oh, such a fine little boy! The finest boy ever born! But the doctor says that Frances will die. She's been sick with consumption all these months."

I said, "What did Mr. Hindley say?"

"I think he cursed," she said. "He cannot believe she is so sick."

Frances did not believe it, either. But she never left her bed again. One night she was leaning on Hindley's shoulder. She had just told him she was feeling stronger. Then a fit of coughing took her. Hindley lifted her in his arms. She put her hands about his neck. Then her face changed, and she died.

Hindley did not cry or pray. Instead, he cursed God and man. He threw himself into drinking.

I took care of the baby, a sweet child named Hareton. As long as the baby was well and quiet, Hindley was happy to leave him with me.

Hindley became so awful that no one could bear to stay at Wuthering Heights. All the servants left, except for Joseph and me. The curate stayed away. No nice people came to visit, except for Edgar Linton. He came to see Miss Catherine.

Catherine was 15 then. She was the queen of the countryside. And what a proud and stubborn thing she was.

But she did not show her rough side to the Lintons. They were always kind and gentle with her. And she was smart enough to copy their good manners. Isabella liked her very much. And she won Edgar's heart and soul.

Catherine's feelings for Heathcliff were still deep. But Hindley's cruel treatment had made its mark. At 16, Heathcliff was a sad and angry young man. He said very little, even to Catherine. He seemed almost to *want* to drive people away.

One afternoon, Hindley was away from the house. Catherine had invited Edgar to visit. When Edgar arrived, I took little Hareton and a dustcloth into the room. Mr. Hindley had told me to stay with the two young people while he was out. So I began to dust.

Catherine stepped behind me. In an angry whisper, she said, "Take yourself and your dustcloth away. Servants don't clean the room when people come to visit!"

"This is a good time to dust," I said loudly. "The master hates me to clean when he's in the room. I'm sure Mr. Edgar will not mind."

Catherine thought Edgar could not see her. She grabbed the cloth from my hand and pinched me—very hard.

I cried out, "Oh, Miss, that's a nasty trick! You have no right to hurt me!"

Catherine's ears were red with anger. She said, "You lie! I never touched you!"

"What's this, then?" I said. I showed her the purple mark.

She slapped me on the cheek.

Little Hareton was sitting near me on the floor. He cried out, "Bad Aunt Catherine!"

She picked up the little boy and shook him so hard he turned pale. Edgar took hold of Catherine's hands in order to stop her. She pulled one arm free and hit him on the ear!

Edgar stepped back. He looked quite shocked.

I grabbed Hareton away from Catherine and carried him into the kitchen. I left the door open so I could see what would happen next.

Edgar took his hat and walked to the door.

Catherine said, "You must not go!"

"I must and I will," Edgar said in a low voice.

Catherine said, "No, not yet, Edgar Linton. You will not leave me feeling this way. I'll be terribly sad all night. And I don't want to be sad because of you!"

Edgar said, "You've made me afraid and ashamed of you. I'll not come here again."

Catherine said, "Well, go, if you like. And now I'll cry myself sick!" She dropped down on her knees and began to cry.

Edgar walked outside. Then he stopped and looked back through the window. He could not leave. He turned quickly and went back into the house.

When I came in later, I saw that their fight had only drawn them closer. They were no longer just friends. Now they were speaking of their love for each other.

I told them Hindley was coming. He was drunk and wild—and ready to pull the house down around our ears.

# 6 A Marriage Proposal

When Edgar heard Mr. Hindley was coming, he left quickly. Catherine ran to her room. I went to hide Hareton. I also made sure the bullets were out of Mr. Hindley's gun. None of us were safe when Hindley was drunk.

Hindley came in, full of curses. He saw me putting Hareton in the kitchen cupboard. Hareton was so afraid of his father that I could hide him anywhere. The poor child would stay quiet no matter where I put him.

Hindley picked up the carving knife and grabbed me by the skin of my neck. He said, "At last I've found it out! Now I know why Hareton is never around. I'll make you swallow the carving knife, Nelly! Don't laugh. I've just thrown the doctor into the marsh. Now I want to kill some of you!"

I didn't believe that Hindley was serious. But there was no telling what he might do. I decided to humor him. "There will be plenty of time for that later," I said. "Why don't you put that knife down and have something to eat?"

He put down the knife and opened a bottle of brandy. He poured himself a glass.

I tried to grab the glass from his hand. I said, "No, don't, Mr. Hindley! Think of your poor son."

"Anyone can take better care of him than I can," he shouted. Then he began to drink and told me to leave him alone. I went out the door. Heathcliff was standing there. He had been listening to Hindley.

Heathcliff said, "It's too bad he can't quickly kill himself with drink. He's trying to, but he's strong. The doctor says Hindley will live longer than anyone this side of the village."

I took Hareton into the next room. I thought Heathcliff had walked out to the barn. But it turned out that he was only on the other side of the room. He had lain down on a bench, where no one could see him.

I began rocking Hareton on my knee. As I sang him a song, Catherine came in.

She said, "Are you alone, Nelly?"

"Yes, Miss," I said.

I began to sing again. I had not forgotten what Catherine did to me a short while ago.

Catherine came and sat at my feet. She looked up at me with those eyes of hers. That look can turn off anger, even when you have a good reason to be angry.

She said, "Nelly, can you tell me something? I

want to know what I should do. Edgar has asked me to marry him. I said yes. Please, Nelly, tell me if I was wrong!"

"Do you love Mr. Edgar?" I said.

She said, "Who can help it? Of course I do."

"Why do you love him?" I asked.

She said, "Well, because he is young and handsome, and happy. And because he loves me. And he will be rich. I will be proud to have such a husband."

"Those are all bad reasons," I said. "Is that why you are afraid it would be wrong to marry Mr. Edgar?"

She said, "I feel in my heart and soul that it is wrong. Once I had a dream that I was in heaven. But it seemed that heaven was not my home. I cried and cried. The angels were so angry they threw me back on earth. I woke up and cried because I was so happy. This is why it seems wrong to marry Edgar.

"I have no more business to marry Edgar than I have to be in heaven. If Hindley had not brought Heathcliff so low, I would never think of marrying Edgar. But it would degrade me to marry Heathcliff now.

"He will never know how much I love him. And it's not because he's handsome, Nelly. It's because he's more myself than I am. Whatever souls are made of, his and mine are the same. But my soul and Edgar's are as different as snow and fire."

Before she finished speaking, I saw that Heathcliff had been in the room. He had listened until Catherine said it would degrade her to marry him. Then he had walked out without a sound. Catherine was turned toward me. She did not see him leave.

"When you marry Mr. Edgar, you will be separated from Heathcliff," I said. "And he will be alone in this world."

She said, "Separated! No one can separate me from Heathcliff. No one would dare to try! You believe I'm thinking of myself. But I'm thinking only of Heathcliff. But if I married him, we would have no money at all. If I marry Edgar, I can help Heathcliff. I can free him from Hindley's power."

I said, "With Edgar's money, Miss Catherine? I don't think so. And that is the worst reason yet for marrying Mr. Edgar."

She said, "It is the best! If anything happened to Heathcliff, the world would be a stranger to me. So don't talk about us being separated. I cannot bear it."

Then Joseph came in and our talk was ended. I went to make dinner. When it was time to eat, Heathcliff did not come to the table. I called, but

there was no answer. I told Catherine he had heard part of what we said.

She jumped up and ran outside. She stood near the road that led from the house. There, she waited. It began to rain, and a wild wind beat about the house. But she would not come in. She called and listened and cried.

It was very late when at last she came in. She would not change her wet clothes. She sat up all night long. In the morning, she cried and cried. Then she became wild. I was afraid she was going mad. We sent Joseph to Gimmerton for the doctor. The doctor told us Catherine was terribly sick with fever.

We took care of her, Hindley and Joseph and I. We were not very gentle with her, I'm afraid. And she did not make it easy for us. But she lived.

Old Mrs. Linton came many times to see her. She said Catherine must come stay with her to get well. So as soon as Catherine was out of danger, she left for Thrushcross Grange. But poor Mrs. Linton must have been sorry she ever invited Catherine. Both she and her husband caught Catherine's fever and died very quickly.

After that, Catherine came back to us. She was more stubborn and bold than ever. The doctor had said she must not become upset. So Hindley let her have her way. He wanted her to make the family proud—by marrying Mr. Edgar.

After his parents died, Edgar brought Catherine to the little chapel in Gimmerton. Like so many young grooms before him, he thought he was the happiest man on earth

In the meantime, we hadn't heard from Heathcliff. There hadn't been a word since the night he ran away.

I had to go with Catherine to Thrushcross Grange. I did not want to leave Wuthering Heights. My little Hareton was five years old. I was just beginning to teach him his letters. But Catherine said I must come with her. So, feeling very sad, I kissed Hareton good-bye. Since then he has been a stranger to me.

At this point in her story, Mrs. Dean looked at the clock. She was quite surprised to see it was half past one in the morning. Saying she must not stay a second longer, she quickly told me good night and went downstairs.

# 7 Heathcliff Returns

The very next day I woke up sick. I felt very weak and I ached all over. What a fine way to begin my new life! Worst of all, the doctor said I might not be able to leave the house until spring.

One day four weeks later, I was finally feeling a little better. I was not strong enough to read, but I wanted to hear more of Mrs. Dean's story.

I rang for her. She was happy to sit down and tell me more.

Mrs. Dean began:

Miss Catherine and I came to live at Thrushcross Grange. I was surprised and happy at how well she behaved. She seemed to care for Edgar Linton almost too much. And she was very kind to Isabella. Of course, both Edgar and Isabella took care never to make her angry.

For a while, I think Edgar and Catherine were quite happy. But their happiness didn't last.

One September evening, I was bringing a basket of apples to the house. I stopped at the kitchen door to look at the moon.

A voice behind me said, "Nelly, is that you? Look

at me. I'm not a stranger."

I looked at the deep, dark eyes. I remembered those eyes. They were Heathcliff's.

"What?" I said. "You've come back? Is it really you?"

"Where is she?" he said. "Is she here? Go—tell her someone from the village wants to see her."

I went in. Edgar and Catherine were sitting together. They looked quiet and happy. I did not want to say anything. But at last I told Miss Catherine someone had come to see her.

Catherine went downstairs. A few minutes later, she flew back up. She threw her arms around Edgar's neck. She said, "Oh, Edgar! Heathcliff's come back—he has!" She pulled him even closer.

Edgar said, "Well, don't strangle me for it! *I* never thought he was so wonderful."

I brought Heathcliff upstairs. Catherine ran to him. She took both his hands and led him up to Edgar. She pushed both Edgar's and Heathcliff's hands together.

I got a better look at Heathcliff now. I was surprised at the change in him. He was tall and strong-looking. Edgar seemed small next to him. Heathcliff was well-dressed, too. He looked proud, and moved and spoke like a gentleman. But there was still something savage about him. His eyes were like black fire.

*45*

The three of them sat down. Catherine's eyes were fixed on Heathcliff. And Heathcliff's eyes flashed with joy. But Edgar was not at all happy.

Catherine said to Heathcliff, "Tomorrow I will think this is a dream! To have seen you and touched you once more. But you have been cruel, Heathcliff. You have been gone three years. And you have never thought of me!"

Heathcliff said in a low voice, "I have thought of you—more than you have thought of me. I had a plan: to have one look at your face. Then I would get even with Hindley. After that I would stay free from the law by killing myself. But seeing you has put this plan out of my mind. No, you will not drive me away this time. I've had a hard life since I saw you last. But I've thought only of you!"

Edgar's face had gone pale with anger. He said, "Catherine, we will have cold tea if we do not go to the table now."

Tea lasted a very short time. Catherine could not eat or drink. Edgar spilled his tea.

Heathcliff did not stay long. As he was leaving, I asked him if he would stay in the village.

Heathcliff said, "No, I am staying at Wuthering Heights. Hindley asked me to stay."

Hindley asked *him*! I thought about this a long time after Heathcliff had gone. I had the feeling that Heathcliff should have stayed away.

Later I asked Catherine why Heathcliff was staying at Wuthering Heights. She said, "Heathcliff stopped by Wuthering Heights that morning. He thought I still lived there. Hindley had some people with him. They were all playing cards.

"Heathcliff joined the game, and Hindley lost money to him. Hindley saw that Heathcliff had a lot of money, so he asked Heathcliff to come again. Then Heathcliff said he would pay very good money to stay at Wuthering Heights. Hindley thinks he can take some of Heathcliff's money away from him. But Hindley should not trust Heathcliff. Not after being so cruel to him."

In the days that followed, Catherine was very sweet and loving to Edgar. He began to feel a little better about Heathcliff's visits. But soon he had a new worry. His sister Isabella had fallen in love with Heathcliff.

Edgar hated the idea of his sister loving a man like Heathcliff. And he knew well what would happen if he did not leave a son behind when he died. Thrushcross Grange would go to Isabella—and her husband.

Catherine told Isabella she was a fool. She said, "If you give Heathcliff your heart, he'll crush you like a bird's egg."

I had to agree with her.

"Heathcliff's not the one for you, Miss Isabella,"

I said. "You should ask yourself where he got all his money. Why is he staying with Hindley, whom he hates? They say Hindley does nothing but drink and play cards. He has been borrowing money on his land. Hindley has gotten worse and worse since Heathcliff came."

But Isabella would not listen. The next time Heathcliff came to Thrushcross Grange, he saw Isabella alone in the yard. I saw him go up to her. Then—he kissed her!

I told Mr. Edgar what I had seen. He was terribly angry. He told me Catherine was to blame for what had happened. He said to me, "This is too much! Call two of the men servants. We will get rid of this Heathcliff!"

Edgar went downstairs to the kitchen. Catherine was there, talking to Heathcliff. Edgar had told me to have the men wait in the hall.

Edgar walked up to Heathcliff. He said, "I am asking you to leave. If you don't leave in three minutes, you will be thrown out."

Heathcliff said, "Catherine, this lamb of yours is acting like a bull!" Then he turned to Edgar and said, "Mr. Linton, I'm sorry you're not worth knocking down!"

Edgar nodded to me. It was a sign to go get his men. I went out to the hall, but Catherine followed me. When I tried to call the servants, she pulled me back into the room. Then she slammed the door and locked it.

Catherine turned to Edgar. "That was not fair!" she said. "You only acted bravely when you had men to back you up!" Edgar tried to pull the key from her hand. But she threw it into the fire. Edgar began to shake. He sank back into a chair and covered his face.

Catherine said, "Don't worry! Heathcliff will not hurt you. You are not even a lamb. You are more like a baby rabbit!"

Heathcliff pushed Edgar's chair with his foot. Edgar jumped to his feet and he hit Heathcliff very hard on the neck. Then he dashed out of the room.

Catherine turned to Heathcliff and said, "You must leave—and quickly! He'll be back with guns and half a dozen men."

Heathcliff said, "No! I won't leave until I crush him like a rotten nut!"

Then I told a small lie. "He's not coming!" I said. "But three servants are on their way. Each one has a heavy stick."

Heathcliff had second thoughts. He took a poker from the fireplace. He hit the lock with the poker, broke it, and went out.

Catherine took me upstairs. She said, "If you see Edgar, tell him I could be terribly sick. He has upset me so! I want to scare him. He is being mean and jealous about Heathcliff. I won't be able to keep Heathcliff as my friend. So I'll break both their hearts by breaking my own."

I didn't want to go along with her plan, so when I saw Edgar coming upstairs, I said nothing.

Edgar came into the room. He said, "There is something I need to know, Catherine. Will you give Heathcliff up? Or will you give me up? I must know which one of us you choose."

Catherine said, "I *need* to be left alone! Don't you see I cannot even stand up? Edgar, you—leave me!"

She hit her head against the sofa, again and again. She ground her teeth.

Edgar looked scared. He told me to bring water. But Catherine would not drink. Her body became stiff, and her eyes turned up. Her face looked like death.

In my heart, I was worried. But I told Edgar what Catherine had said about wanting to frighten him.

Catherine heard me. She gave me a wild look, and then got up and ran away from us. She locked herself in her room. The next morning, she would not eat.

Edgar spent his time reading. He did not ask how Catherine was.

# 8 Brain Fever

Three nights later, Catherine unlocked her door and asked me for something to eat. Then she climbed back into her bed. She said she was dying. I thought she did look sick. And she talked in a strange way. But I felt she still was trying to scare Edgar. I said nothing.

"What is Edgar doing?" Catherine said. "Is he sad? Is he dead?" I said, "He is well, I think. He spends a lot of time reading his books."

I should not have said these things. But I didn't know how sick she was. I still felt that part of her sickness was just an act.

Catherine said, "Reading his books! And here I am dying! If I were sure it would kill him, I would kill myself now! These three awful nights, I've never closed my eyes!"

Then she became wild. She turned and tossed about. She tore the pillow with her teeth. Then all at once she was like a quiet child. She pulled the feathers from her pillow one by one. She said, "That one is a turkey feather. And this is a wild duck's, and that is a pigeon's."

Then she slid out of bed. Before I could stop her,

she opened the window. The night air of winter cut about her face like a knife. I tried to pull her away. But her madness made her too strong for me.

"Look!" she said. "There's the graveyard. Heathcliff and I used to dare each other to stand by the graves. We'd ask the ghosts to come out. Heathcliff, if I dare you now, will you come? I won't lie there by myself. I won't rest until you are with me!"

Edgar came in. He had heard our voices as he passed by. I cried, "Oh, help me, sir! She is sick, and I can do nothing with her!"

"Catherine is really sick?" he said. He looked at Catherine's face. All at once, he was terribly afraid. He took her in his arms.

I went for the doctor. On my way to the road, I passed by the garden. There I saw something moving in the dark. It was Miss Isabella's little dog, Fanny. The dog was hanging by its neck. It was almost dead.

As quickly as I could, I let the dog loose. I thought I heard the sound of horses running away from the house. But I had other things to think about just then.

I got to the village just in time to catch the doctor as he was going out. He came back with me to the house. He said Catherine would probably live. But her mind might never be the same.

Mr. Edgar and I were up all night with Catherine. Early that morning, a servant girl ran into the room. She said, "Mr. Edgar! The young lady—"

Edgar said, "Not so loud. What's the matter with Miss Isabella?" The girl said, "She's gone, she's gone! Heathcliff's run off with her! They stopped at the blacksmith's shop in Gimmerton. They needed a shoe for one of the horses. And the blacksmith's daughter saw them. The woman had a cloak around her face. But then she wanted a drink of water. And while she drank, the cloak fell back. And it was Miss Isabella!"

Edgar sent me to look in Isabella's room. It was

empty. I went back to Mr. Edgar. I said, "Will you try to catch them, sir? And bring them back?"

Edgar said, "She went because she wanted to. Now she is my sister only in name. But not because I have disowned her. She has disowned me."

Isabella and Heathcliff stayed away two months. During those months, Catherine was terribly sick with brain fever. Edgar stayed with her day and night. How happy he was when the doctor said she would live! But she would never be strong again.

In the spring, she was well enough to leave her room. We hoped very much she would get better. We hoped this not only for Catherine, but because she was going to have a baby. If the baby was a boy, Thrushcross Grange would belong to him one day, and not to Heathcliff.

Soon after Isabella ran away, she wrote Edgar a letter. But he did not write back, so she wrote to me. In the letter, Isabella told me that she would give the world to see Edgar's face again. She said that her heart came back to Thrushcross Grange 24 hours after she left it.

Then Isabella asked, "Is Mr. Heathcliff a man? If so, is he mad? And if he is not mad, is he a devil?"

Isabella told me what happened when she got to Wuthering Heights. The first person she saw was Hareton. He was a strong-looking little boy wearing dirty clothes. She remembered that Hareton was Edgar's nephew. She went to shake hands with him. But he told her to go away or he would tell the dog to go after her. Isabella left him alone and quickly walked across the yard.

Next, Isabella met Hindley. He was also very dirty. His long, shaggy hair almost covered his face. It was late, and Isabella was very tired. She asked Hindley where Heathcliff's room was.

Hindley said, "Joseph will show you Heathcliff's room. And be sure you lock it!"

"But why?" said Isabella. She did not like the idea of locking herself in with Heathcliff.

Hindley said, "Look here!" He showed her a strange gun. A double-edged spring knife was attached to the barrel. Hindley said, "Every night I look to see if Heathcliff's door is locked. If he ever leaves it open, he's done for! I have many reasons not to kill him. But I can't help wanting to!"

Isabella looked at the gun. An awful feeling came over her. What power she would have if that gun were hers! She said, "If you hate Heathcliff so much, why don't you tell him to leave?"

"Heathcliff must not leave!" Hindley said. "I must get my money back from him. Or my son Hareton will grow up with no money at all."

Isabella left him. Joseph showed her to Heathcliff's room, but it was locked. Joseph would not help her find another place to sleep. At last, she fell asleep in a chair in the hall.

Heathcliff woke her up. He told her Catherine was sick. He said Edgar was to blame. And since he could not hurt Edgar, he would make *her* cry as often as he could.

Isabella ended her letter. She said, "I do hate Heathcliff. I am terribly sad. I was a fool! Do come to see me. I will wait for you every day."

# 9 Two Broken Hearts

I went to see Mr. Edgar. I told him how much Isabella missed him. But he only had cold words for her. I felt very sad as I walked to Wuthering Heights.

How the house had changed! It was dirty and dusty now. And Isabella had changed, too. Her pretty face looked tired. Her hair was half up and half down. Heathcliff was there, too. And I must say *he* never looked better.

Isabella came up to me. She held out her hand. She thought I would have a letter from Edgar. But I had none. She looked as if she wanted to cry.

Heathcliff asked me about Catherine's illness. I said, "Catherine will live. But she will never be the same again. Edgar takes very good care of her, because he remembers the way she used to be. And because he is so kind."

Heathcliff said, "Because he is so kind! Do you think I can leave Catherine to a man like that? A man who takes care of her because that is a *kind* thing to do? I must see her! I *will* see her!"

I said, "You must not, Mr. Heathcliff. If you and Edgar have another fight, that would kill her."

Heathcliff said, "I do not have to see Edgar at all. But you must help me. I wish I knew how much Catherine cared for Edgar. If she only cared a little, I could tear his heart out. But if it would hurt Catherine to lose Edgar, I would die before I touched a hair on his head! Edgar can love her with all his weak power. But he could not love her in 80 years as much as I love her in a day!"

Isabella said, "Catherine and Edgar care for each other very much. You must not talk about my brother this way!"

Heathcliff said, "Listen to her, Nelly. Isabella is tired of me already. But I never lied to her. I never pretended to love her. When she and I left Thrushcross Grange that night, I hanged her little dog. And I told her I wanted to hang everyone in Thrushcross Grange, except one person. She thought *she* was that one person. But now, at last, she knows me. And, at last, she hates me."

Isabella said, "Nelly, don't tell Edgar or Catherine one word of this. Heathcliff says he has married me to have power over Edgar. But he won't! I will die first! I hope he will get angry enough to kill me. My greatest wish is to die, or to see him dead!"

Heathcliff said, "That is enough. Go upstairs! I wish to speak to Nelly alone."

She left. Then Heathcliff said, "I have no pity! I want to hurt them—more and more!"

I put on my hat.

Heathcliff said, "Put that down! You must let me see Catherine. You must tell me when Edgar is out. If you don't, I'll come with a gun. I'll fight my way in. But wouldn't it be better if you'd let me in when she's alone?"

I said, "You must not see her. She is not strong. The surprise would be too much for her. If you insist on coming, I shall have to tell Mr. Edgar about your plan."

Heathcliff said, "Then I'll keep you here! And I will see her without your help."

Well, I must have told Heathcliff *no* 50 times. But in the end, I went home with a letter to give to Catherine. I am afraid I did the wrong thing. But I did not know what else to do.

I kept the letter in my pocket for three days. I knew Heathcliff was hiding and waiting, outside the house. But I did not want to give Catherine the letter until Edgar was out.

That Sunday, Edgar went to church. I went up to Catherine's room. She was sitting near the window. She wore a loose, white dress. She looked beautiful. But her beauty was not of this world. It seemed she was getting ready to leave this life—and soon.

She read the letter. But she was too ill to understand what it meant. I heard footsteps in the hall. Heathcliff came in.

He bent down to Catherine and took her in his arms. As soon as he saw her, he knew she was going to die. He kissed her, again and again. He could not bear to look at her face. He said, "Oh, Catherine! Oh, my life! How can I bear it!"

Catherine said, "What now? Heathcliff, you and Edgar have broken my heart. I will not pity you. You have killed me—and now you look so strong!"

Heathcliff tried to stand up. But Catherine held him by his hair.

She said, "I wish I could hold you until we were both dead! How many years will you live after I am gone? Will you forget me? Will you love others after me?"

Heathcliff pulled his head free. He stood up and walked to the other side of the room. He ground his teeth and said, "Don't do this to me! I have not broken your heart—you have broken it yourself! And you have broken my heart, as well. You loved me—then what *right* had you to leave me for that fool Edgar? Nothing should have parted us, but you did it of your own free will. And now every word you say will burn into me after you are gone! When you are at peace, I will be in hell! Isn't that enough for you?"

"I shall not be at peace," sobbed Catherine. All at once, she was taken by a fit. Her heart was beating very hard. When it was over, she said,

"Heathcliff, I only wish we would never be apart. Now, you must forgive me. Won't you come to me again?"

She got up, holding on to the back of the chair. His eyes flashed at her. They were wet with tears. Quickly, she went to him. He pulled her close and held her fast.

Catherine's eyes closed. I was afraid she had fainted. I went to her. But Heathcliff showed his teeth to me, like a mad dog. He pulled her even closer to him.

Catherine opened her eyes. She put her hand about his neck. He kissed her wildly.

I was getting very worried. Mr. Edgar would be back soon, so I told Heathcliff he must leave. He cursed. Still he held Catherine tight. She never moved.

Soon I saw the servants coming into the yard. Mr. Edgar was close behind them. I said, "Now he is here! Hurry down! If you leave by the front stairs, no one will see you!"

Heathcliff said, "I must go, Catherine. But I'll wait by your window. I'll see you again."

Catherine cried, "No! Oh, don't—don't go. It is the last time! Heathcliff, I will die! I will die!"

Heathcliff said, "Hush, my darling! Hush, hush, Catherine! I'll stay, even if he shoots me."

I heard Mr. Edgar on the stairs. I was full of horror. I said to Heathcliff, "She doesn't know what she is saying! You better go now," I cried.

Mr. Edgar heard me and began to run up the stairs. I saw that Catherine's head hung down. She had fainted—worse, maybe she was dead.

Edgar ran to Heathcliff. His face was full of surprise and anger. But Heathcliff lifted Catherine and put her into Edgar's arms.

Heathcliff said, "Look! Unless you are a devil, take care of her first. Then speak to me." He walked into another room and sat down.

Mr. Edgar and I did what we could for Catherine. At last she opened her eyes again. But she did not know who we were. Edgar had forgotten about Heathcliff. But I did not. As soon as I could, I went to him and told him he must leave. I said I would let him know the next morning how Catherine was.

"I will go outside," he said. "But I will stay in the garden. You better come see me tomorrow, Nelly, under those trees. Or I will come back in again, whether Edgar is here or not."

# 10 "May She Never Know Peace!"

About twelve o'clock that night, Catherine gave birth to a baby girl. Mr. Lockwood, this is the girl you saw at Wuthering Heights. She was a weak, little, seven months' child. Two hours after the birth, Catherine died. She died with a smile on her lips. No angel could have looked more beautiful.

Soon after the sun came up the next morning, I went to find Heathcliff. He was waiting under a tree in the garden. I was afraid to tell him Catherine was dead.

But he said, "She's dead! I found that out already. . . . Don't cry! She doesn't want your tears!" Then he began to shake a little. He said, "How did she die?"

I said, "Quietly. Her life closed in a gentle dream. May she wake in peace in the next life."

Heathcliff said, "May she never know peace! Why, she's a liar to the end! Where is she? Catherine, may you not rest as long as I am alive! You said I killed you. Then haunt me, as a ghost. But do not leave me here, where I cannot find you. I will not bear it! I cannot live without my life! I cannot live without my soul!"

He hit his head against a tree—hard. He left blood on the tree trunk. He cried out, not like a man, but like a hurt animal. He told me to leave him. I was afraid for him, but I went away.

The evening after the funeral, it began to snow. Edgar kept to his room. I was taking care of the baby, whom they had named Cathy.

All at once the door opened. It was Isabella. Her light silk dress was wet from the snow. A cut under her ear dripped blood. She was out of breath.

"I've run away!" she cried. "Please order a carriage to take me to the village. And tell a servant to bring me some clothes."

Then she pulled off her wedding ring. She took a poker from the fire and hit the ring with it, again and again. Then she threw the ring into the fire. She said, "There! Heathcliff can buy me another, if he gets me back again. He might come after me, just to get back at Edgar. I wish I could stay here. But Heathcliff would never let me. He could not bear to see me or Edgar happy!"

I helped Isabella change her clothes. Then she told me about her last day at Wuthering Heights.

Isabella said, "Hindley and I were in the kitchen. Heathcliff was just coming home. But all at once Hindley got up and locked the door so that Heathcliff could not get in. He turned to me and said, 'Heathcliff has done us both great wrong. We

need to punish him. Are you as soft as your brother? Or do you dare to help me?'

"I said, 'I would be happy to teach Heathcliff a lesson, but we must not hurt him. Violence is like a spear with points at both ends. Those who use violence get hurt worse than their enemies.'

" 'Violence is a just return for violence!' Hindley said. 'I'll ask you to do nothing, but hold your tongue. My actions will help you, in spite of yourself. And this will help Hareton, too. It's time to make an end!' He pulled out the gun with the knife attached. Then he reached over to put out the candle.

"I grabbed the candle away. I said, 'I'll not hold my tongue!' I ran to the window. I called, 'You had better keep away, Heathcliff! Hindley will shoot you!'

"All at once Heathcliff burst through the window. He grabbed Hindley's arm. The gun went off and the knife sprang back. It went deep into Hindley's arm. Hindley passed out from the pain.

"Heathcliff took Hindley's head and banged it on the stone floor. He kicked him again and again. But he did not kill him.

"After a while, Hindley came to. Heathcliff told me not to say a word. He then told Hindley that he had hurt himself while he was drunk.

"The next morning, I came down to the kitchen. Hindley was there. He was terribly sick. Heathcliff was also there. He didn't look up. His face was like stone, and terribly sad.

"I could not miss this chance to hurt Heathcliff. I said, 'Now I see how much Hindley looks like Catherine. He has her eyes. Only you, Heathcliff, have made them black and red. I know what would have happened if Catherine had been a fool and married you. You would have made her eyes look like Hindley's!'

"Heathcliff grabbed a dinner knife. He threw it at me. It hit me here, below the ear. Hindley grabbed him. The two men fell to the ground, fighting. I ran out the door and on to Thrushcross Grange."

Isabella had finished her story. Her clothes were ready to go. She kissed me and got into the carriage. She took the little dog Fanny with her. She never came back here. She was too afraid of Heathcliff. But she and Edgar wrote often. He was very happy when Isabella left Heathcliff.

She made a new home near London. There, she had a son, whom she named Linton. When she left, we had no idea she was going to have a baby.

Mr. Edgar kept very much to himself. He stayed away from the village. He even stopped going to church. But he had his little daughter Cathy to comfort him. She was the queen of his heart.

Six months after Catherine died, Hindley was dead, too. He was not even 27 years old. Joseph told me he had locked himself in the house. Then he spent the whole night drinking. The next day, Joseph and Heathcliff broke in. Hindley was lying on the floor. They could not wake him. They sent for the doctor. But it was too late.

All Hindley's money had been lost to Heathcliff. Now Hareton had no money at all. Since Edgar was Hareton's uncle, the boy should have come to Thrushcross Grange. But Heathcliff would not let Hareton go. He told me that if Edgar took Hareton, he would take Linton from Isabella. So we could do nothing.

# 11 The Crybaby

The next 12 years were happy ones for me. It was a joy to take care of young Cathy and watch her grow. She filled that sad house with sunshine. There never was such a pretty little girl! She had her mother's dark eyes, and the yellow curly hair of her father's family. Her spirit was strong but not wild. Her love was deep and gentle.

She had never been outside the park at Thrushcross Grange. But she asked many questions about the land beyond her home. She wanted very much to see Pennistone Crags. Mr. Edgar told her she must wait until she was older.

About this time, Isabella wrote Edgar. She had been sick a long time. She was afraid she would die soon. She wanted Edgar to come to see her so she could say good-bye. And she wanted to make sure that young Linton would live at Thrushcross Grange and not go to Heathcliff.

Mr. Edgar left for London as soon as he could. He was gone three weeks. Cathy missed him terribly. She would pass the time by riding about on her pony. I never thought she would leave the park. But one day, she was not back for tea.

Right away, I thought of Pennistone Crags. I walked up out of the park and up the hills as quickly as I could. I was afraid she had hurt herself.

Pennistone Crags lay a little beyond Wuthering Heights. As I passed by the house, I saw one of our dogs outside the door.

Zillah, the housekeeper, let me inside. There was young Cathy talking to Hareton. He was now 18, and quite big and strong. He was dressed like a farm boy. He looked at young Cathy with wonder.

I was very happy to see her. But I said, "Well, Miss Cathy! I'm very upset with you. This is your last ride until your father comes back!"

She did not want to leave, but at last I got her out the door. Then she turned to Hareton and said, "Get me my horse."

Hareton's face turned dark with anger. He said, "I'll be damned before I'll be *your* servant!"

Young Cathy's eyes went wide with surprise.

I said, "Those aren't nice words to say to a young lady! Let us go now, Cathy."

Cathy said to Hareton, "How dare you! I'll tell my father what you said. Now get me my horse!"

Zillah said, "There now, Miss. It will not hurt you to be polite. Hareton is your cousin. He was never your servant."

Young Cathy said, "My cousin! That's not true! My cousin is in London. He's a gentleman's son!"

I said, "Hush, Cathy. Hareton *is* your cousin. But if he is not kind to you, you don't have to see him again."

Cathy began to cry. Hareton tried to make peace. He brought her a fine little puppy. But she only looked at him and cried harder.

I believe Cathy had liked Hareton very much when she first met him. It was a sad trip home.

I told Cathy that her father did not like the people at Wuthering Heights. And if he found out that she had been there, he would be terribly angry. He might even tell me to leave Thrushcross Grange. So she gave her word that she would not tell. And she kept it. She really was a sweet little girl.

The day Mr. Edgar came back to Thrushcross Grange, we got a letter edged in black. Isabella was dead. I was told to set up a room for young Linton.

Cathy was very happy she was going to see her "real" cousin. Young Linton was asleep when the carriage pulled up to the house at Thrushcross Grange. He was just six months younger than Cathy. But he was thin and weak-looking.

We brought him into the house. I set him on a chair, but he began to cry. "I can't sit in a chair," he sobbed.

"Go to the sofa, then. And Nelly will bring you some tea," said Mr. Edgar.

Cathy came up to him and kissed his cheek. She

gave him the tea as if she were feeding a baby. He liked this. He dried his eyes and smiled a little.

Mr. Edgar turned to me and said, "Linton will do very well, Nelly. It will be good for him to be around another child. In time, he will grow strong—if we can keep him."

But we could not keep young Linton. Later that night, Joseph came to the house. He said Mr. Heathcliff wanted Linton for himself. We must bring him to Wuthering Heights right away.

Mr. Edgar was very sad. He said to me, "We must not tell Cathy where young Linton has gone. If she finds out, she will want to go to Wuthering Heights to see him. We will tell her only that Linton's father sent for him."

Early the next morning, we put Linton on Cathy's horse. The poor boy did not know what to think. He knew nothing about his father. He was not at all sure he wanted to go to Wuthering Heights.

Heathcliff, Joseph, and Hareton were waiting at the door. Linton looked at them with fear in his face. Heathcliff came up to his son, laughing in an ugly way. He said, "He's worse than I thought, Nelly. Have they given him snails and sour milk to eat?"

"Come here," Heathcliff said to the boy. But young Linton held on to me and cried.

Heathcliff reached out his arm and pulled Linton up to him. He said, "None of your tears! We're not

going to hurt you, Linton—isn't that your name? You are your mother's child, all right. I don't see any of *me* in you."

I said, "I hope you'll be kind to the boy. You are all he has in the world."

"Oh, I'll be kind," Heathcliff said. "I have a good reason to be. Thrushcross Grange will go to Linton. I want to keep him alive until I am sure Thrushcross Grange will go to me. I'll take good care of him. Even though he doesn't look worth it!"

It was time for me to leave. While Linton was looking the other way, I went out the door. But then he saw me and cried, "Don't leave me! I won't stay here! I won't stay here!"

But the door was closed. I got up on the horse and rode away.

We had a hard time with Cathy that day. There were many tears when she found her cousin had gone away. But in time, she even forgot how he looked.

Sometimes when I went to the village, I would see Zillah. I always asked how young Linton was.

Zillah said he seemed to be sick all the time. It was one thing after another. She said, "Oh, he's such a crybaby, that boy. The window must always be shut. I must build a fire for him, even in summer. And he cares only for himself. Never a thought for anyone else."

# 12 Love Letters

We did not see young Linton again until years later—on the day Cathy turned 16. That day, she wanted to see if the birds on the moors had built their nests yet. We walked out toward the moors. I had a hard time keeping up with her.

Soon, we were far from Thrushcross Grange and close to the house at Wuthering Heights. I called to her, but she was too far ahead. When I came over a hill, I saw two men walking up to her. One of them was Hareton. The other was Mr. Heathcliff.

I ran up to them and said, "Miss Cathy, it is getting late. We must go back right away."

But Mr. Heathcliff said to Cathy, "I think it would be better if you stopped to rest at the house. My son is there, and he has met you before. He would be quite happy to see you."

Miss Cathy could not think of who this "son" might be. She wanted very much to see him.

I said, "Miss Cathy, you may not. It's out of the question."

Heathcliff said, "Hold your tongue, Nelly. Hareton, walk Miss Cathy up to the house."

I said, "Miss Cathy, don't!" But as I began to run

after her, Heathcliff grabbed my arm.

"She must not go into the house, Mr. Heathcliff!" I said. "This is very wrong. Now she'll see Linton, and know everything."

Heathcliff said, "I want her to see Linton. I plan to have her fall in love with him and get married."

I said, "But Linton is weak and sickly. If he died, Thrushcross Grange would go to Cathy."

He said, "No, it would not. There is nothing in the will that says so. It would go to me."

We reached the house. Cathy and Linton met each other once again. At 16, Cathy was beautiful, with her gold hair and bright eyes. Young Linton had grown tall. He was very thin and white. But still, he was a good-looking young man.

Cathy wanted to go outdoors again. But Linton would not leave the fire. So Heathcliff made Hareton show Cathy around the grounds.

Hareton was very shy. He did not say a word to Cathy. Then, as they went inside again, she saw the words over the door. She said, "Why is that writing there?"

Hareton said, "It's some damn thing. I cannot read it."

Cathy said, "Can't read it? But it's in English."

Linton heard them. He said, "Hareton can't read. Can you believe he's so stupid?" He began to laugh at Hareton. Cathy laughed, too.

Hareton's face was red with anger. He said to Linton, "If you weren't such a crybaby, I'd knock you down in a minute!" He walked out, very angry and hurt.

Linton told Cathy all about Hareton, saying how stupid he was. Heathcliff watched Linton and Cathy with a mean look on his face.

Then Heathcliff said, "Hareton is worth two of Linton. But Hareton will never have Linton's chances to be happy. I've done a good job of getting even with Hindley. I've brought Hareton even lower than Hindley brought me. And the funny thing is,

Hareton cares a lot for me. I'm the only friend he has in the world."

I had nothing to say to this. Heathcliff laughed in an ugly sort of way.

It was a long time before I could get Miss Cathy away. She could not wait to see Linton again. She would not listen to anything I told her about Heathcliff.

But she did listen to her father. Mr. Edgar told her a little of what Heathcliff had done to Isabella. He also told her how Heathcliff had made Wuthering Heights his own. Cathy knew very little of evil. I believe she was quite shocked by what her father told her.

Later that night, I saw her crying. I asked her what was the matter. She said she felt bad for Linton. She knew he expected her to visit again. She wanted to send him a note.

I told her to forget about Linton. A note would only start things up again.

But a few weeks later, I saw her spending a lot of time with a small box, which she kept locked up. I also saw her talking to the boy who brought milk from the village. One night I took the house keys and found a key that would open the box.

Inside were many letters—from Linton. The first ones were short. His words were shy. But the later ones were long love letters. Some of the things he said seemed to come from an older person. I took the letters out of the box.

The next day, I watched Cathy as she opened the box. She looked inside and said "Oh!" She seemed very surprised. Right away she guessed what had happened. She ran to me and took my hands. She said, "Nelly, you've got them! Please, don't tell my father. Please! I won't write any more. Please, don't tell!"

I said, "If I burn them, will you promise not to send any more?"

She promised. We burned every one of them. Then, very sad and hurt, she went to her room.

The next day the boy came with the milk. I gave him a note to take to Wuthering Heights. It said, "Mr. Linton must send no more notes to Miss Cathy. She will not receive them."

# 13 Secret Visits at Night

That fall, Mr. Edgar became ill. He had to stay in the house all winter. Cathy was very sad and worried about her father. I don't think she thought much about young Linton then.

Mr. Edgar saw how sad she was. He said Cathy must get outside more. So we walked almost every day. One day we were out walking at the edge of the park. Cathy saw some late roses growing at the top of the wall. She climbed up to get them. Her hat fell over the side of the wall. She jumped down to get it. Then she started to laugh. She said, "Nelly, I can't get back up. You must open the door."

I began to look through my keys. I hoped I had one that would open the door.

Just then I heard a horse coming up the road. I said to Cathy, "Who is coming?"

A voice said, "Ho, Miss Cathy! I'm glad to see you. There is something I must talk to you about." The voice was Heathcliff's.

I picked up a stone and beat at the lock with it.

Cathy said, "I won't talk to you, Mr. Heathcliff! My father says you are evil. And that you hate both him and me. And Nelly says so, too."

Heathcliff said, "You can believe what you like about me. But I must tell you that you are breaking young Linton's heart. You stopped writing to him. So now he thinks you care nothing for him. He is dying for you—that is the truth!"

I said, "How can you lie to the poor child? Miss Cathy, don't listen to him!"

At last the lock broke. I opened the door.

Heathcliff looked hard at me. He said, "I tell you that Linton is dying. If you don't believe me, Nelly, come see for yourself. I will be gone for a week. I'm sure Cathy's father would want her to see her cousin."

Then all at once, it began to rain. Cathy and I ran back to the house. When we got inside, I tried to make Cathy believe that Heathcliff was surely lying. But she said she must see for herself.

The next day we set out for Wuthering Heights. It was rainy and cold. My feet got quite wet. By the time we got there, I wished very much we had not come.

Linton was sitting on a chair. When Cathy went up to him, he said, "Don't kiss me. It takes my breath away. Why did you not come? It made me so tired, writing those long letters." He began to cough. He coughed so long it scared me. When the fit of coughing had passed, Cathy brought a pillow for his head.

Linton said, "It's not high enough!"

She brought a second pillow.

Linton said, "Now it's *too* high!"

"But what should I do?" said Cathy.

"Sit down in the chair next to mine. Let me lean on your knee," said Linton. "And you must not talk. But you could sing a song, if you can sing."

She sang many sweet songs. That seemed to make them both quite happy.

Cathy left Wuthering Heights in high spirits. But for me, it was a long, wet trip home.

The next day I was sick with a cold. The cold kept me in bed for three weeks. Every day Cathy took care of both her father and me. But I never asked myself how she spent her evenings. One evening, when I was well enough to go upstairs, I looked into her room. It was empty. None of the servants had seen her.

I sat and waited by the window. After a while, Cathy rode up. I heard her come in, very quietly. When she saw me, she stopped short. She began to cry. And then she told me everything. She had been to Wuthering Heights almost every night while I was sick.

She said, "Sometimes I was happy at Wuthering Heights. It made me happy to have Linton smile, and talk to me. But much of the time he is so cross, Nelly!

"Many nights were sad ones for me. And one night was terrible. As I came up to the house, Hareton stopped me. He pointed to the writing over the door. He said, 'Miss Cathy, I can read that now! It says, "Hareton Earnshaw!" '

"I said, 'And can you read the numbers?'

"He said, 'No, not yet.'

"I said, 'Oh, you really are stupid, aren't you?' "

"Stop, Miss Cathy," I said. "It was very wrong of you to be cruel to Hareton. He was trying to please you. And he is not at all stupid. It's just that Heathcliff won't let him learn anything."

Cathy said, "Well, you will see if he was worth being kind to. I went in to see Linton. He said he was sick, and I must be very quiet and not make him cross. I was going to read to him. But then Hareton burst into the room. He said to Linton, 'Get out of here! And take her with you! You won't keep me out of here! Go!'

"Hareton pulled Linton into the kitchen. I followed them. Then Hareton locked both of us in the kitchen.

"Linton grabbed the handle of the door. He cried, 'Let me in or I'll kill you! I'll kill you!'

"Linton looked awful then, Nelly! His thin face was white. He shook all over. I took his hands. I tried to pull him away, but he began to scream. The noise was terrible. Then he was taken by an awful fit of coughing. Blood burst from his mouth. He fell to the floor.

"Hareton came into the kitchen. He picked Linton up and carried him upstairs. Zillah went up, too. They would not let me come up with them. I cried and cried.

"After a while Zillah came down. She told me Linton was better and I should leave.

"As I was getting on my horse, Hareton came out. He held on to my horse and said, 'Miss Cathy, I'm very sorry. But it's too bad.'

"I was afraid of him then! I slashed at him with my whip and rode away.

"When I arrived the next night, Linton was much better. But he would not talk to me for an hour! When he did talk to me, he said *I* was to blame for the night before! I do feel sorry for him, Nelly. Linton will never let his friends be at ease. And he'll never be at ease himself."

Miss Cathy had finished her story. She hoped very much that I would not tell her father. But I did tell him—as soon as I could.

Mr. Edgar was very upset. He told Cathy she must never go to Wuthering Heights again. But he did say she could write Linton. And Linton could come sometimes to Thrushcross Grange. If Mr. Edgar had known more about young Linton, he may not have let Cathy see him at all. But he did not know what a bad nature young Linton had. And he did not know how sick the boy was.

Mrs. Dean stopped her story for a moment. She said, "I see, Mr. Lockwood, that you smile when I talk about Miss Cathy. But of course, you have met her. And who could see Miss Cathy and not love her? And why have you asked me to put her picture in your room?"

"Stop, Mrs. Dean!" I said. "I do believe I could love Miss Cathy. But could she love me? And my home is not here. I belong to the busy world of London. And I must go back to it. But, please, Mrs. Dean, go on with your story."

# 14 Locked Inside the Room

Mrs. Dean went on:

Mr. Edgar was afraid he would not live much longer. He thought a lot about what would happen to Cathy after he was gone. He asked me about young Linton.

I said, "He is not strong, sir. I think he will die in a few years. But I can say this: Linton is not like his father at all. If Cathy married him, I think she could control him."

Edgar said, "If Linton can make Cathy happy, I don't care if he is Heathcliff's son! But if he is only a weak tool of Heathcliff's, then Cathy is better off alone."

Mr. Edgar wrote Linton. He asked him to visit Thrushcross Grange. But Linton said Heathcliff would not let him come. He asked if Cathy could meet him on the moors. Of course, Cathy wanted very much to see young Linton again. So at last, Mr. Edgar said yes. His illness had gotten much worse in the last few days. He knew now that he would die very soon. He wanted Cathy to stay at Thrushcross Grange after he died. And the only way this could happen was for her to marry Linton. We did not know that Linton was dying almost as quickly as he was.

The day came for us to meet young Linton on the moors. We rode to the spot—a marker stone. But Linton was not there. When we found him at last, we were very close to Wuthering Heights.

Linton was lying on the grass. He got up when he saw us. But he walked quite slowly. He looked very sick.

I said, "Mr. Linton! You are not well! You should be in bed!"

Young Linton said, "Oh, no! I'm better—better!" He looked afraid.

Cathy said, "I cannot believe you really wanted to see me. Why did you ask me to come when you are so sick? I think we should go."

Linton began to cry. He said, "No! You must not go. Please stay, Cathy. I will be killed if you go. I'm a coward. A coward and a traitor. But you said you loved me once. Don't leave me!" He sat down on the grass again.

Cathy said, "What is the matter? Why are you so afraid? You wouldn't do anything to hurt me, would you, Linton?"

Linton said, "I cannot tell! I'm so afraid of him!"

Cathy said, "All right, don't tell. I'm not afraid!"

Just then Mr. Heathcliff walked up to us. He said, "Nelly, what is happening at the Grange? I hear Edgar is dying. Is this true?"

I said, "Yes, I'm afraid it is."

Heathcliff said, "Well, this boy seems to want to die before Edgar does. What's this? He's crying! How long has he been acting like this?" He turned to Linton. He said, "Get up! Get up right now!"

Linton looked quite scared. He tried to get up. But he was too weak. He said, "Stay with me, Cathy! Help me back to the house."

Cathy helped him up. She whispered, "Linton, dear, I can't go to Wuthering Heights. My father will not let me. . . . Heathcliff won't hurt you. Why are you so afraid?"

Linton cried, "I can't go back to that house! I can't go back without you!"

So Cathy helped Linton back to the house. I couldn't stop her. And how could she have told him no?

We came to the door and went into one of the rooms inside. Cathy helped Linton to a chair. Then Heathcliff suddenly locked the door of the room.

Cathy looked at Heathcliff. Her eyes were wide. She jumped up and tried to grab the key. She said, "I won't stay here! I won't!"

Heathcliff held the key tight. Cathy pulled at his fingers. Then she bit his hand.

Heathcliff grabbed her. He slapped her again and again—very fast and hard—on the side of her head.

I ran up to him. I cried, "You villain! You villain!"

He pushed me back. He knocked the breath out of me.

The fight was over in two minutes. Heathcliff let go of Cathy. He went out, and Cathy began to cry.

I turned to young Linton. I said, "You know what your father is going to do. Tell us!"

Linton said, "Give me some tea, and I'll tell you."

I gave Linton a cup of tea. He drank some of it. Then he looked at Cathy and said, "Father wants us to be married. He knows your father would not let us get married now. And he's afraid I might die. So we must be married tomorrow morning. You have to stay here all night. Then, if you do what father wants, you can go home the next day."

Cathy was terribly upset. She said, "I cannot stay here! What will my father think?"

Linton sat back and drank his tea. I did not like him at all just then. Now that he was safe from his father's anger, he was happy.

Heathcliff came back. He took Linton out of the room and left us alone. We looked for a way out of the room but there was none. We sat and waited for the night to pass.

In the morning, Heathcliff opened the door. Quickly, he pulled Miss Cathy out. Then he locked me inside again.

For five days, I stayed in the room. The only person I saw was Hareton. He brought me food, but he would tell me nothing.

# 15 "She's My Wife Now."

After five days, Zillah opened the door. She was surprised to see me. She said there was a story in the village that Miss Cathy and I had been lost in the marsh. Everyone thought we were dead.

I asked about Miss Cathy, but Zillah knew nothing. I ran downstairs. There was Linton. He was lying down, sucking on a piece of candy.

"Where's Miss Cathy?" I said.

"She is upstairs and she must stay there," he said. "Even if she cries herself sick. My father says it's wrong for her to want to leave me. After all, she's my wife now."

I said, "Don't you remember how kind she has been to you? How can you be so cruel to her? She wants so much to see her father. He will not live much longer."

"I know he will die soon," said Linton. "Father says so. And I'm glad. Father says Cathy only married me for my money. But now Thrushcross Grange will be mine, and not hers. Now everything she has is mine. I'm tired now, Nelly. Go, go away!"

I left him and went back to Thrushcross Grange. By now, Mr. Edgar was very close to death. I told him Mr. Heathcliff had kept us locked up at Wuthering Heights. I said very little about Linton. I did not want Mr. Edgar to worry too much about Cathy. I told him Cathy would come home that night.

Mr. Edgar was not sure what Heathcliff was going to do. But he told me to send for the lawyer, Mr. Green. He wanted to change his will. He wanted to make sure everything would go to Cathy.

I sent a servant to the village to get Mr. Green. Then I sent four men servants to Wuthering Heights to bring Miss Cathy back. I made sure they had weapons.

The first servant came back from Gimmerton alone. He said Mr. Green was busy, but he would come later. Then the four men came back without Cathy. Mr. Heathcliff had told them she was too sick to leave.

I told the men they had been fools. I thought I would send more men—many of them—the next day.

But that night, Cathy herself arrived. Linton had let her go free at last. She went upstairs to see her father. I told her she must say she was happy with young Linton. And she said she would do so.

I went upstairs and waited outside the door. After a while, I went in.

Mr. Edgar's face was very happy. He kissed

Cathy's cheek. He said, "I am going to your mother. And you, sweet child, will come to us later." And then he died.

Cathy sat in the room all that night and part of the next day. She did not cry. I believe her tears had all been spent.

Later that night, Mr. Green came. But he would do nothing for us. He had sold himself to Mr. Heathcliff.

Heathcliff left Miss Cathy alone until after the funeral. Then, that evening, he came for her. He walked in without knocking. The house was his now.

"Get your things, Cathy," he said. "And no more running away. Linton will not help you again. Hurry now! Get upstairs."

Cathy said. "I won't run away. I'll stay with Linton. He is all I have now." Then she went upstairs. She seemed very tired and sad.

"Mr. Heathcliff," I begged, "let Cathy and Linton stay here. You hate them both. You will not miss them."

But Mr. Heathcliff said no. He wanted to rent Thrushcross Grange. Then I asked if I could change places with Zillah. But he would not hear of it.

Then Heathcliff said, "Yesterday the sexton was digging Edgar's grave. I gave him good money to knock the side of Catherine's coffin off. Not Edgar's side, damn him! I will be buried on the other side.

And when I die, the sexton will knock the side of my coffin off, too. Our dust will mingle and Edgar's spirit will never be able to tell us apart."

I said, "Mr. Heathcliff, that was very wrong. You must let the dead rest in peace!"

"Peace?" he shouted. "For 18 years she has given me no peace—until last night. Last night I had a dream that I was dead. And she lay close to me at last."

Just then Cathy came downstairs. She whispered to me, "Good-bye, Nelly. Come and see me. Don't forget."

Heathcliff said, "Nelly will *not* come to see you. I want no spies at Wuthering Heights."

Soon after, I did go to Wuthering Heights. But Joseph wouldn't let me in. I learned from Zillah that Linton was dead. His illness had gotten worse and worse. But Heathcliff wouldn't spend money for a doctor. Cathy shut herself up in Linton's room and took care of him herself. Long days and nights she spent there. Then at last, one night he died.

After Linton was buried, she stayed in that room alone for two weeks. Heathcliff came to see her only once. He showed her young Linton's will. The will left everything to Heathcliff. Cathy had nothing.

When it got too cold to stay in the room, Cathy spent her days downstairs. But she kept to herself. She would not talk to Hareton or Zillah. She turned them away with tears and angry words.

When I heard all this, I wanted to leave Thrushcross Grange. I thought I could get a small house. I could have Miss Cathy come live with me. But I soon gave up the idea. I knew Heathcliff would never let Cathy be free.

Nelly Dean's story was at an end. I was feeling much better now. I decided that in a day or two, I would go to Wuthering Heights. I would tell Mr. Heathcliff that he could find someone else to rent Thrushcross Grange. I had decided to go back to London. I didn't want to spend another winter here.

When I got to Wuthering Heights, Hareton came to the gate. What a handsome young man he was. It was too bad he drove people away.

Mr. Heathcliff would not be home until dinner, so I went inside to wait. Cathy was there, working in the kitchen. I gave her a note from Mrs. Dean. But Hareton took it from her. He said Mr. Heathcliff should see it first. Cathy turned her face away. She wiped her eyes.

Hareton watched her. Then he threw the note down at her feet.

Cathy picked it up and read it quickly. She said to me, "Please tell Nelly that I cannot answer. I have nothing to write with. I don't even have a book to tear a page out of."

"No books!" I said. "How can you live here without them?"

She said, "Mr. Heathcliff got rid of my books. But there are a few left." Cathy turned to Hareton. She said, "I know you have them, Hareton. You took them, even though you cannot use them. You took them the way a magpie takes silver spoons—just for the fun of taking them!"

Hareton turned red. He went out of the room. Soon he came back with several books. He threw them in Cathy's lap.

He said, "Take them! I never want to read or hear or think of them again!"

Cathy said to me, "I hear Hareton trying to read to himself. You should hear how he sounds!"

She opened a book. She began to read in a slow way, like a beginner.

Hareton could take no more. He slapped her face. Then he threw the books into the fire.

Just then Heathcliff walked in. He said, "What is the matter, Hareton?"

"Nothing, nothing!" Hareton answered. He walked quickly outside.

Heathcliff watched him go and said, "Every day I look for Hindley in him. But I see *Catherine* more in him every day! It hurts me to look at him."

He did not seem to see me. He looked a little strange. And he seemed thinner, too. I went up to

him and said hello. Then I told him I would be leaving Thrushcross Grange.

He asked me to stay and eat. It was not a happy dinner. Heathcliff was quiet. Hareton said nothing. Cathy was not there at all. Heathcliff made her eat in another room with Joseph.

As I left, I thought, "How sad life is in that house! What a fairy tale it would be if Cathy and I got together. And we both went away to the busy life of the city!"

# 16 Young Lovers

In September of 1802 I was invited to the moors by a friend. I was making the long trip to his house, when I found I was very close to the village of Gimmerton. It was early in the day. But I had to spend the night somewhere. So I thought I may as well stay at Thrushcross Grange.

To my surprise, Nelly Dean was not there. An old woman was taking care of the place. She told me that Mrs. Dean was at Wuthering Heights. So I walked across the moors to that unhappy house.

Even before I walked in the door, I knew that Wuthering Heights had changed. The gate was not locked, but open. The smell of flowers was in the air. As I walked by a window, I heard voices.

One voice, as sweet as a silver bell, said, "That's not right! Say it right, or I'll pull your hair."

The man's voice was soft and deep, "The word is 'contrary,' then. Now kiss me, for getting it right."

She said, "No, you must read it all over again."

As I watched through the window, the young man began to read. I could see that he was well dressed and quite good looking. His face was very happy as he bent over the book.

The young woman stood close to him, her hand on his shoulder. Her shiny gold curls touched his brown hair. How beautiful and happy she looked.

I bit my lip. How sad I was. I had thrown away any chance I had with her.

The young man finished reading. Then he wanted at least five kisses for his work. After that, the two of them came to the door. They were going to walk on the moors.

I knew well enough that Cathy and Hareton would not want to see me right now. I went around to the kitchen, feeling very low.

Mrs. Dean was there. She was sewing and singing a song. She was very surprised to see me. I told her I wanted to stay at Thrushcross Grange for the night.

Mrs. Dean said, "Then you must see Miss Cathy."

I wasn't sure what to make of this.

Nelly said, "Ah! Then you have not heard that Mr. Heathcliff died?"

"Heathcliff died? When?" I said.

"Three months ago," she said. "But do sit down, Mr. Lockwood. Let me take your hat, and I'll tell you all about it."

Mrs. Dean began:

I came to Wuthering Heights two weeks after you left, Mr. Lockwood. I am not sure why Mr. Heathcliff wanted me there. But Zillah had left, and Mr. Heathcliff said he was tired of seeing Cathy. He wanted me to set up a room for myself, and keep Cathy with me.

I was happy to come. But the house kept me very busy. I had little time for Miss Cathy. And often she had no one to talk to.

By and by she began to try to talk to Hareton. I think she was sorry she had been so cruel to him. One day Cathy tried to give Hareton a book of hers. But he would not come near it.

Cathy went up to Hareton. He kept looking at the fire. She said, "Now I'm glad you're my cousin, Hareton. I just wish you weren't so cross with me."

"Go away!" Hareton said.

"I won't," Cathy said. "I don't hate you, Hareton. Come. You are my cousin, after all."

Hareton said, "I won't have anything to do with you! You and your damned tricks!"

Cathy began to cry. She said, "You hate me! You hate me as much as Mr. Heathcliff does!"

Hareton said, "You're a damned liar! I took your side! I've made him angry a hundred times, taking your side!"

Cathy began to dry her tears. She said, "I didn't know you ever took my side. I always felt so sad and angry at everybody. But now I thank you. And I ask you to forgive me. What else can I do?"

She put out her hand to him. Hareton sat still, looking at the floor.

Then she bent down and kissed his cheek. After that, Hareton did not know where to turn his eyes.

Cathy wrapped up a handsome book in white paper. She wrote on the paper, "To Mr. Hareton Earnshaw." Then she gave it to me. She said, "Tell Hareton that if he takes it, I'll teach him to read it. And if he won't take it, I'll go upstairs and never bother him again."

I put the book on Hareton's knee. Cathy waited. In a few minutes she could hear Hareton tearing off the paper.

She ran over to him. "Will you be my friend now, Hareton?" she said.

"No," he said. "You will be ashamed of me, every day of your life."

She said, "So you won't be my friend?" She came closer. Her smile was sweet as honey.

Soon they were bent over the book. Cathy's hand was on Hareton's shoulder.

They grew to love each other. It did take time. Hareton didn't change in a day. And Cathy wasn't always patient. But they both wanted to please each other. And they did.

So you see, Mr. Lockwood, it wasn't so hard to win young Cathy's heart. But now I'm glad you didn't try. When Hareton and Cathy marry on New Year's Day, it will be the crown of all my wishes.

At first, Heathcliff was terribly angry that Cathy had made friends with Hareton. But very soon after that, he told me he didn't care anymore.

Heathcliff said, "It's funny, Nelly. I worked so hard to hurt Hindley and Edgar and their children. I wanted their power and their money. And I have won everything. But now I don't care. It's too much trouble to even lift my hand to hit them."

He went on, "There's a strange change coming, Nelly. My life means almost nothing now. I forget to eat and drink. I almost have to tell myself to breathe—and my heart to beat."

We did not see Mr. Heathcliff for days. Then one morning, we saw him walking about the house. We all wondered at him, for he looked quite wild and happy.

That afternoon, he asked me for dinner. I set it down in front him. He took up his knife and fork, then laid them back on the table. He looked out the window as if he saw someone outside. But there was no one. He got up and walked out. As he walked past me, I heard his breath. It was as fast as a cat's.

After an hour or two, he came back inside. How strange he looked! His eyes were full of joy. His body shook like a cord held tight.

I said, "Mr. Heathcliff. Tell me why you are acting so strangely. Where have you been? I've been worried. . . ."

He said, "Last night I was at the door of hell. Today I can see heaven! I have my eyes on it. It's not more than three feet away! . . . . And now you had better go."

Heathcliff came and went. I couldn't get him to eat again. And he never seemed to sleep. One night as I passed his room, I heard him walking about. He was talking in a low voice. The only word I could catch was "Catherine."

The next night was the same. I could hear him walking and groaning the whole night. I sent for the doctor. But Heathcliff wouldn't let him into the room. Heathcliff said he was feeling better. But he wanted to be left alone.

The night after that it rained. In the morning, I was outside the house. I saw Heathcliff's window swinging open and the rain driving in.

I found another key to his room. Mr. Heathcliff was in bed—on his back. His eyes met mine. They looked alive and fierce. He seemed to be smiling. I didn't think he was dead. But I touched his hand. It was cold! I tried to close his eyes, but I couldn't. All at once I was afraid. I ran from the room.

His death upset me terribly. I thought of the past, and all the sad things that had happened.

We buried Heathcliff as he had wanted—next to Catherine. Everyone in the village of Gimmerton was shocked.

I hope Mr. Heathcliff sleeps in peace. But some people around here swear that they have seen his ghost walking on the moors. One evening I was going to Thrushcross Grange when a little boy came up to me. He was crying.

I said, "What's the matter, little man?"

He said, "Heathcliff is over there—with a woman. And I don't dare pass them!"

I said nothing about it, but I told the boy to take the other road. Then I went on my way.


Mrs. Dean stopped talking as the gate swung open. Hareton and Cathy were coming back from their walk. All at once, I felt I had to leave. I said good-bye to Mrs. Dean. I went out through the kitchen.

Before returning to Thrushcross Grange, I walked toward the village. I stopped when I reached the church. There I found three graves. Catherine's was in the middle. Edgar and Heathcliff were on each side of her. I stood there watching the moths that fluttered among the flowers. I listened to the soft wind that blew through the grass. And I wondered how anyone could ever believe the three of them were not at peace in that quiet ground.